JOHN RUTTER

VISIONS

SOLO VIOLIN PART

MUSIC DEPARTMENT

OXFORD
UNIVERSITY PRESS

SOLO VIOLIN

VISIONS

JOHN RUTTER

1. Processional and prelude: Jerusalem the blessed

Urbs Je - ru - sa - lem be - a - ta, Di - cta pa - cis vi - si -
O Je - ru - sa - lem the bless - ed, Vi - sion that can nev - er

- o,_____ Quae con - stru - i - tur__ in cae - lis Vi - vis ex la - pi - di - bus,
fade;_____ Built of liv - ing stones in hea - ven, There in splen - dour bright dis - played;

Et an - ge - lis co - ro - na - ta, Ut spon - sa - ta co - mi - te._____
Crowned in_____ glo - ry__ with God's an - gels, As a roy - al bride ar - rayed._____

Por - tae__ ni - tent mar - ga - ri - tis Ad - y - tis pa - ten - ti - bus:_____
Decked with__ pearl her__ gates re - splen - dent Wide are o - pen ev - er - more;

Et vir - tu - te me - ri - to - rum Il - luc in - tro - du - ci - tur_____
By God's grace and in - ter - ces - sion Faith - ful souls may thi - ther soar._____

Om - nes__ qui ob Chri - sti no - men Hic in mun - do pre - mi - tur.
All who__ in Christ's name have suf - fered, Those who earth - ly tri - als bore.

OXFORD UNIVERSITY PRESS MUSIC DEPARTMENT, GREAT CLARENDON STREET, OXFORD OX2 6DP

2. Arise, shine

shine;____ for thy light____ is come,____ and the glo - ry of the

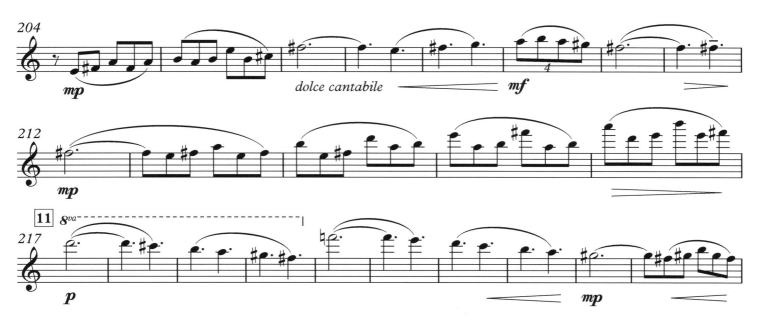

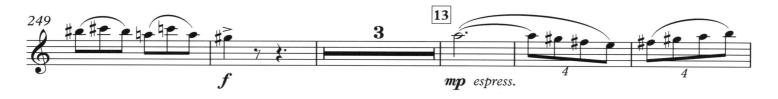

14 **Andante con moto** ♩ = ♩. of preceding

rall.

3. Lament for Jerusalem

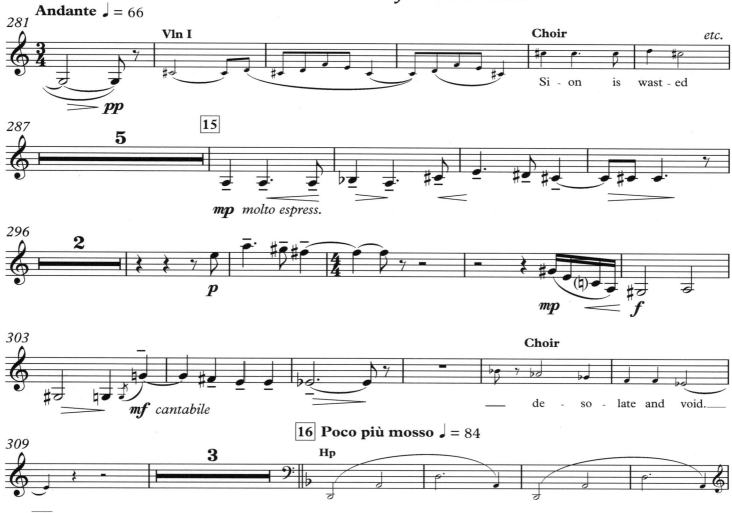

V.S.

317

324

330
17

336

343

350 18   pochiss. rit.

a tempo
356

361

19
366

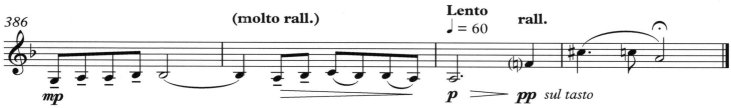

4. Finale: The holy city

poco stringendo

a tempo, poco più mosso ♩ = 84 poco rall.

Choir

Lamb is the light, the Lamb is the light, the light,_____ is the light,_____ the light there‑of.

Tempo I ♩ = 63

poco rit.

Hp

p ethereal *mp*

a tempo (♪ = 126 – a little slower than in Mvt. 1)

p *pp*

(♩ = ♩ of preceding = 63)

poco rit. al fine

Vlns (or Organ)

p *dim.* *pp*

Cello Time Joggers

a first book of very easy pieces for cello

Kathy and David Blackwell

Illustrations by Alan Rowe

Welcome to the Second Edition of **Cello Time Joggers**. You'll find:

- open string pieces and tunes using the finger pattern 0-1-34
- duets—start with the staves marked ☆; come back and play the other part later
- one new piece, replacing no. 3
- audio play-along tracks for all pieces (including scales and Super Sprinter exercises) available to download from www.oup.com/ctjoggers2e or to access on principal streaming platforms
- scales and arpeggios in the keys of G, D, and C major, one octave
- piano and cello accompaniments available separately in printed collections
- An ideal book to use alongside *Cello Time Starters*

OXFORD

UNIVERSITY PRESS

Open Strings

C G D A

crotchet (quarter-note)

crotchet rest (quarter-note rest)

minim (half-note)

minim rest (half-note rest)

dotted minim (dotted half-note)

whole bar rest (whole measure rest)

1. Bow down, O Belinda

American folk tune

Printed in Great Britain

OXFORD UNIVERSITY PRESS, MUSIC DEPARTMENT, GREAT CLARENDON STREET, OXFORD OX2 6DP

2. Under arrest!

KB & DB

Count 2 bars

pizz.

Four short crot-chets played on G, *(rest)* one fell off and left just three. *(rest)*
Four short quar-ter-notes on G,

7

1 2 3, *(rest)* 1 2 3, *(rest)* one fell off and left just three. *(rest)*

Say the word '*rest*' quietly to yourself as you play.

3. Someone plucks, someone bows

Traditional
Words KB & DB

pizz.

arco

Down, up goes the bow, when we're play-ing fast or slow;

3

down, up goes the bow, when we're play-ing high or low.

4. Down up

KB & DB

Down up A string, down up D string, down up G string, down up C string;

Play the D and end with G.

*

* Fill in the letter names of these notes.

5. Hill an' gully rider

Trad. Jamaican

6. Fast lane

Try even faster the second time through!

7. In flight

KB & DB

In the rests, let your bow make a circle as you swoop and soar like a bird.

5

8. Lift off!

Rock

KB & DB

Lift your bow off in each of the rests and let it orbit! (Make a circle with your right arm.)

Rhythm game:

Or - bit round the moon.   (etc.)

9. Katie's waltz

Count 4 bars

KB & DB

Gently

1st Finger

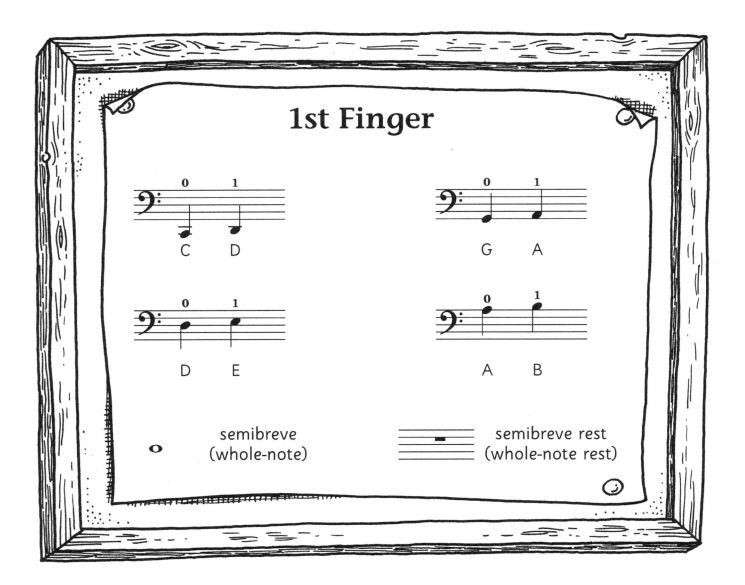

semibreve
(whole-note)

semibreve rest
(whole-note rest)

10. Copy cat

KB & DB

Can you play what I play? G G A A

Can you play what I play? Play it now with me.

Can you play what I play? D D E E

Can you play what I play? Play it now with me.

8

11. Rhythm fever

Count 2 bars

KB & DB

Rock tempo

Rhy-thm fe-ver, 1 2 3 4 feel the beat, 1 2 3 4

7

feel the rhy-thm, 1 2 3 4 in your feet. 1 2 3 4 Feel the rhy-thm

12

as you play it, feel the beat go 1 2 3 4 Rhy-thm fe-ver,

16

1 2 3 4 rhy-thm fe-ver, 1 2 3 4 rhy-thm fe-ver, oh yeah!

12. Here it comes!

KB & DB

Through the teeth and past the gums, so watch out, tum-my, here it comes!

5 *

9

Through the teeth and past the gums, so watch out, tum-my, here it comes!

* Think of a foody rhythm and play it on these notes.

Here is an idea to start you off:

Fish and chips and ice cream.

9

13. Tap dancer

KB & DB

Steadily

*Tap the cello with your left-hand fingers.

14. So there!

Count 4 bars

KB & DB

Brightly

So there!

15. Rowing boat

KB & DB

16. Ally bally

Scottish folk tune

11

17. C string boogie

KB & DB

With a gentle swing
pizz.

Spin your cello around! *

* Be careful!

18. Travellin' slow

KB & DB

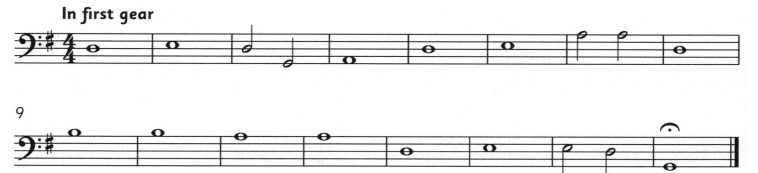

In first gear

19. Tiptoe, boo!

KB & DB

Count 2 bars

Spookily

Tip-toe tip-toe   tip-toe, boo! (*etc.*)

9

15

21

Boo!
(shout)

Also try playing this pizzicato.

20. Lazy cowboy

KB & DB

At a gentle trot

9

3rd Finger

quavers
(eighth-notes)

21. Off to Paris

French folk tune

14

22. City lights

KB & DB

23. Clare's song

KB & DB

Count 4 bars

When you can play slurs, come back and play this piece slurring three crotchets (quarter-notes) to a bow.

24. Phoebe in her petticoat

American folk tune

Swap parts when you do the repeat.

25. Peace garden

KB & DB

Not too fast

26. Summer sun

KB & DB

27. On the prowl

KB & DB

28. Knock, knock!

KB & DB

18

29. Ready, steady, go now!

KB & DB

30. Happy go lucky (for Iain)

KB & DB

Count 4 bars

Try the harder part of 'Someone plucks, someone bows' on page 3.

4th Finger

slur

31. Algy met a bear

KB & DB
Words anon.

mf

Al - gy met a bear, a bear met Al - gy. The

mf

bear was bul - gy, the bulge was Al - gy!

Swap parts when you do the repeat.

Try the harder part of 'Off to Paris' on page 14.

20

32. Listen to the rhythm

KB & DB

Lis - ten to the rhy - thm on my big cel - lo. Crot-chets sound like
Quar - ter - notes like

this: Crot-chets sound like that!
this: Quar - ter - notes like that!

Lis - ten to the rhy - thm on my big cel - lo. Mi - nims sound like
Half-notes sound like

this: Mi - nims sound like that!
this: Half-notes sound like that!

Lis - ten to the rhy - thm on my big cel - lo. Se - mi - breves like
Whole-notes sound like

this: Se - mi - breves like that!
this: Whole-notes sound like that!

33. Cattle ranch blues

KB & DB

Try the harder part of 'Hill an' gully rider' on page 4.

34. In the groove

KB & DB

Count 2 bars

22

35. Stamping dance

Czech folk tune

36. Walking bass

KB & DB

37. Chopsticks for two

KB & DB

24

38. Runaway train

Count 4 bars

KB & DB

Express train tempo

39. Distant bells

Count 2 bars

KB & DB

40. Lazy scale

KB & DB

41. The old castle

With a singing tone

KB & DB

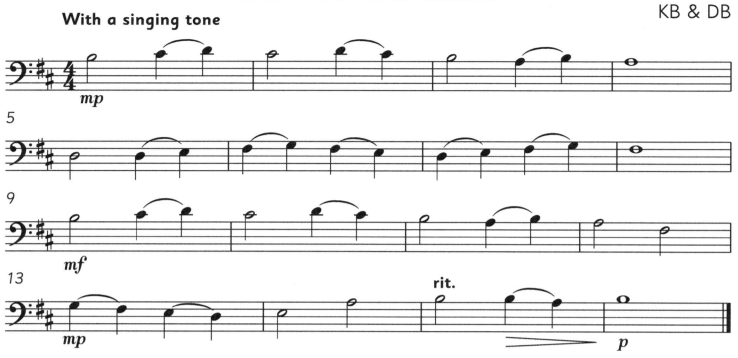

42. Rocking horse

KB & DB

Count 4 bars

Gently

Try playing 'Clare's song' on page 15, slurring three crotchets (quarter-notes) to a bow.

43. Patrick's reel

KB & DB

Try the harder part of 'Ally bally' on page 11.

44. Calypso time

Count 2 bars

KB & DB

Try the harder part of 'Bow down, O Belinda' on page 2.

45. Cello Time

Count 4 bars

KB & DB

Scales and Scaley Things!

Playing scales and arpeggios with different rhythms is a great way to brighten up your practice.

Try each note of these scales and arpeggios with this rhythm:

Ready steady go now

Football teams, your friends' names, your favourite animals, and food can all be starting-points for your own rhythms. Make up some more patterns of your own.

G major scale

G major arpeggio

Add the arpeggio fingering like a telephone number below.

D major scale

D major arpeggio

C major scale

C major arpeggio

30

Super sprinter

KB & DB

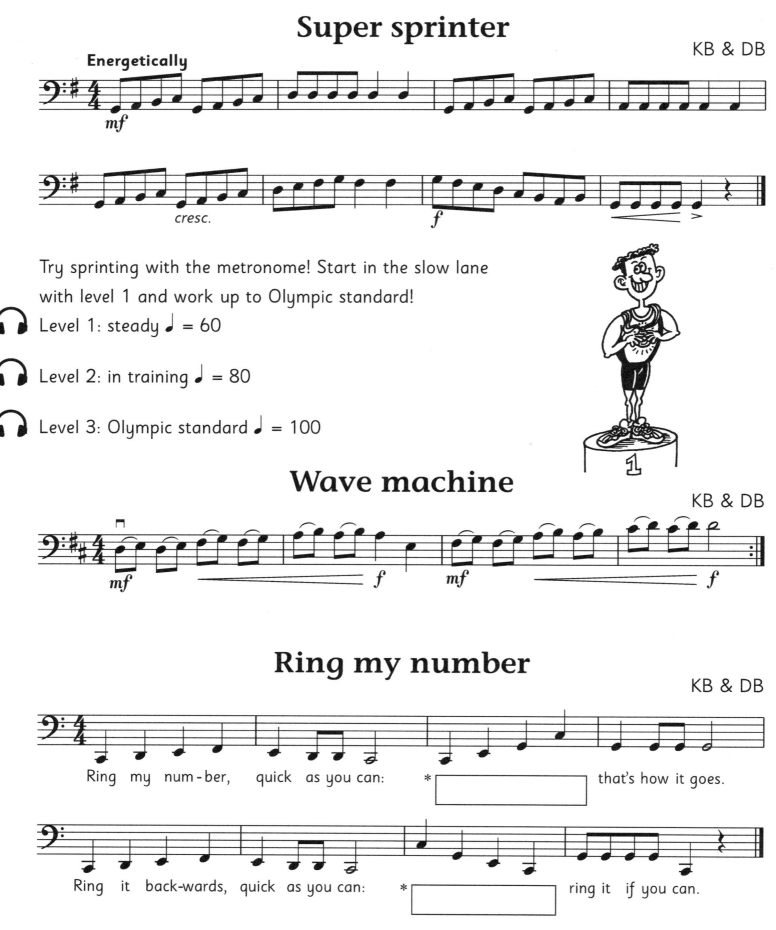

Try sprinting with the metronome! Start in the slow lane with level 1 and work up to Olympic standard!

Level 1: steady ♩ = 60

Level 2: in training ♩ = 80

Level 3: Olympic standard ♩ = 100

Wave machine

KB & DB

Ring my number

KB & DB

Ring my num-ber, quick as you can: * [   ] that's how it goes.

Ring it back-wards, quick as you can: * [   ] ring it if you can.

* Use the empty boxes to write in the fingers needed to play these notes.

Challenge: can you play this tune starting on the G or the D string?

Music Fact-Finder Page

Here are some of the words and signs you will find in some of your pieces!

How to play it

pizzicato or pizz. = pluck
arco = with the bow
⊓ = down bow
V = up bow
> = accent
 = tremolo

Don't get lost!

‖: :‖ = repeat marks

┌1.┐ ┌2.┐ = first and second time bars
Play the first bar first time through; skip to the second bar on the repeat
D.C. al Fine = repeat from the beginning and stop at **Fine**
D.℀ al Fine = repeat from the sign ℀ and stop at **Fine**
rit. = gradually getting slower
a tempo = back to the first speed
⌢ = pause

Volume control

p (*piano*) = quiet
mp (*mezzo-piano*) = moderately quiet
mf (*mezzo-forte*) = moderately loud
f (*forte*) = loud
ff (*fortissimo*) = very loud

━━━━━━━ or *crescendo* (*cresc.*) = getting gradually louder
━━━━━━━ or *diminuendo* (*dim.*) = getting gradually quieter

ISBN 978-0-19-351319-8

9 780193 513198